First Published by Evans Brothers Limited
2A Portman Mansions,Chiltern Street, London W1U 6NR,
United Kingdom

Copyright © Evans Brothers Limited 2005

This edition published under license from Evans Brothers
Limited

North America edition published by Chelsea Clubhouse,
a division of Chelsea House Publishers and a subsidiary of
Haights Cross Communications
2080 Cabot Boulevard West, Suite 201, Langhorne,
PA 19047-1813

United States Copyright held by Chelsea House Publishers

A Haights Cross Communications Company

Printed in China

Library of Congress Cataloging-in-Publication Data
applied for.

ISBN 0-7910-8179-6

Acknowledgments

The author and publishers would like to thank the following
for their help with this book:

Jordan and Amanda Fey; Kate Easdale and the KEBBA
Black Belt Academy and Bowplex, Longwell Green,
Bristol, UK.

Thanks also to the UK National Deaf Children's Society for
their help in the preparation of this book.

All photographs by Gareth Boden

Credits

Series Editor: Louise John
Editor: Julia Bird
Designer: Mark Holt
Production: Jenny Mulvanny

LIKE ME LIKE YOU

Jordan Has a
HEARING LOSS

JILLIAN POWELL

CHELSEA CLUBHOUSE
An Imprint of Chelsea House Publishers
A Haights Cross Communications Company
Philadelphia

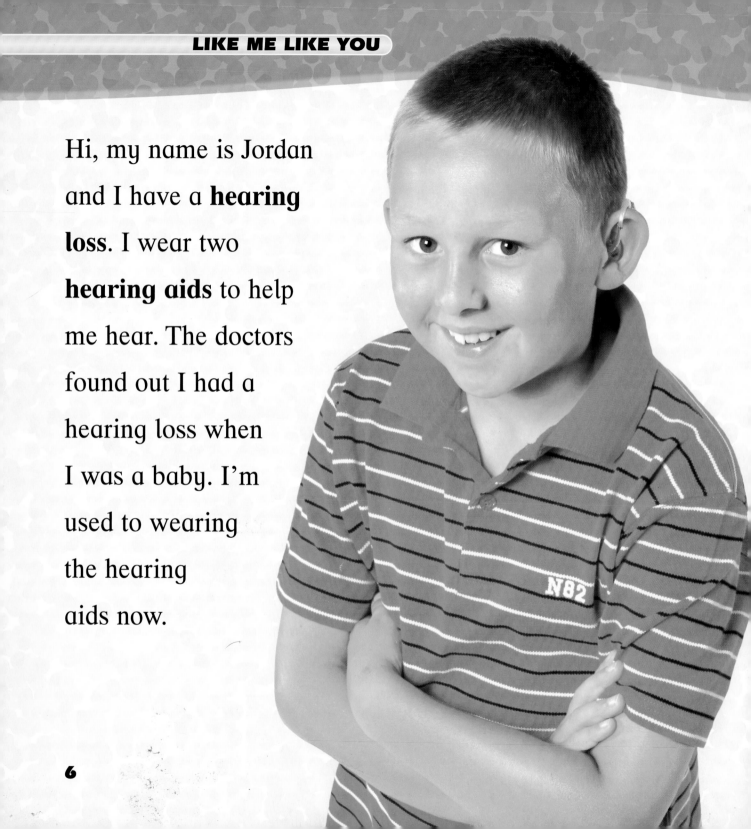

Hi, my name is Jordan and I have a **hearing loss**. I wear two **hearing aids** to help me hear. The doctors found out I had a hearing loss when I was a baby. I'm used to wearing the hearing aids now.

HEARING LOSS

About one or two children in a thousand are born with a hearing loss. Others can develop hearing loss after a serious illness.

I live at home with Mom and my sister Jessica. I love soccer and often play with my friends. I also like swimming, playing on the computer, and riding my bike.

I wear my hearing aids all the time. The only time I take them off is when I go to bed, and when I'm taking a shower or swimming. This is because I must not get them wet.

I like going to the movies. When I go, I flick a switch on my hearing aids so that I can hear the sound better through the loop system there.

LOOP SYSTEMS

Loop systems help hearing aids make sounds clearer by cutting out background noise.

I use a special alarm clock. I put it under my pillow, and in the morning it shakes to wake me up.

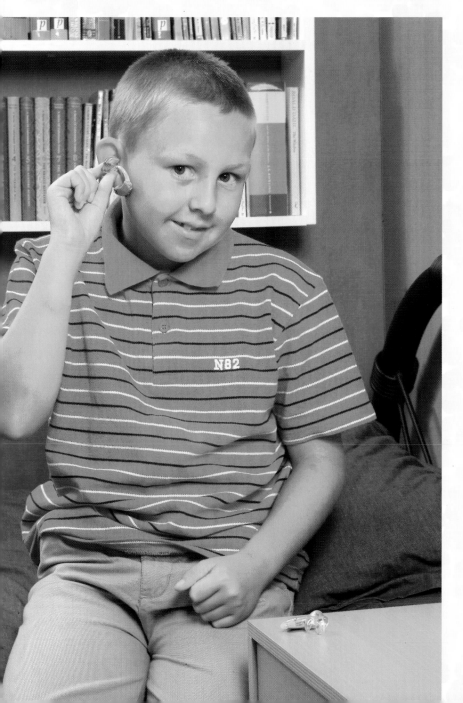

When I wake up, I put my hearing aids on right away. Then I can hear Mom telling me it's time to get ready for school!

While we're having breakfast, the telephone rings. Mom tells me it's for me. I push a special button on the phone to make it louder. It's my friend Alex, asking if I'm coming to **karate** today.

I go to karate class once a week. It's a lot of fun. I get my karate stuff ready, then Mom tells me it's time to go.

Kate is our karate teacher. There are lots of children in our class and some of them have a hearing loss like me. We stand at the front so we can hear and see Kate better and copy what she's doing. This is how we start the class.

Sophie and Maddy have a **profound** hearing loss. They talk and understand by using **sign language.** They use their hands to sign different words and ideas. Their faces help them show what they're saying.

SIGN LANGUAGE

Many people who have a hearing loss use sign language to talk and understand.

15

Today, Kate wants us to practice our kicks. First she tells us what she wants us to do. Then she tells us again, using sign language so Sophie and Maddy can understand. She tells us to keep our knees up and our toes back.

16

We all take turns to practice our kicks with a partner. I'm practicing with Alex.

We play games at karate, too. This is my favorite game. It's called Stuck in the Mud. My team is chasing everyone else. Alex and the girls have blue belts. I have a white belt, because I'm still a beginner.

When we're playing games it can get really noisy! Sometimes I turn my hearing aids down so it's not so bad. When I do this, my friends let me know what's happening by tapping me on the shoulder and speaking to me clearly.

Then we take a break. Sometimes Sophie and Maddy show us how to say something in sign language. I've learned to sign "My name is Jordan."

FINGERSPELLING

Fingerspelling uses the fingers and hands to stand for different letters of the alphabet.

Today, they're teaching me some of the **fingerspelling** alphabet. I try spelling out my name.

The class is over for another week. Mom's here to pick me up. I want to get home quickly because there's a soccer game on the television and my favorite team is playing!

When I watch television, I wear a headset that lets me make the sound louder so I can hear better. It works from a box in front of the television. Before I had the headset, the television was sometimes too loud for everyone else.

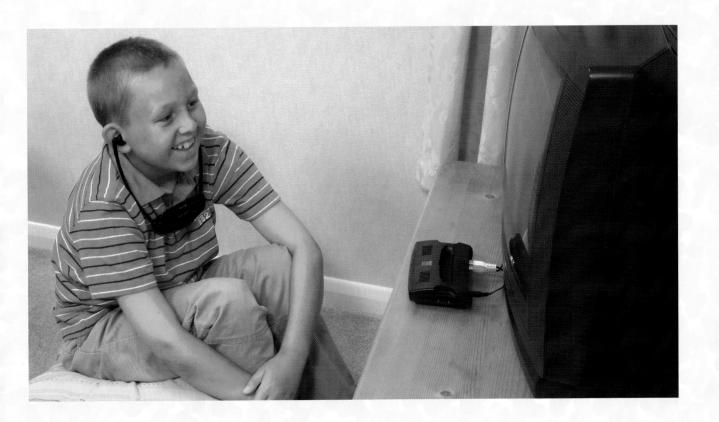

Mom is calling my teacher to remind her I'll be a little late to school tomorrow. I have to go to the hospital to have my hearing test. I have a hearing test twice a year. I have to listen for sounds and play a game to show when I hear something.

I have a **radio aid** to wear in school. It helps me hear my teacher better, even when she's on the other side of the classroom. She wears a **microphone** and when she speaks the sounds are sent to my radio aid, then into my hearing aids.

Some days my hearing is worse than others and it's harder to hear what someone is saying when it's noisy. But I've learned to **lip read** by watching people's mouths when they're speaking.

LIP READING

Lip reading means watching the shape of the lips when someone is talking. It can help someone with a hearing loss to understand the words being spoken.

Having a hearing loss doesn't stop me from doing all the things I enjoy, especially my favorite thing — going bowling with my friends!

27

Glossary

Hearing aid a small aid worn in or behind the ear that makes sounds louder

Hearing loss when someone finds it difficult to hear some sounds, like Jordan

Fingerspelling using the fingers and hands to stand for different letters of the alphabet

Karate a Japanese art of self-defense

Lip reading watching the lips to read the words being said

Microphone something you speak into that makes sounds louder

Profound hearing loss when someone finds it difficult to hear many sounds, like Sophie and Maddy

Radio aid an aid worn on the body that sends radio waves that are turned into sound waves

Sign language using hands, body, and face to show words, thoughts, and ideas

Index

Further Information

American Society for Deaf Children (ASDC)
800-942-2732
www.deafchildren.org
Support, encouragement, and information for families raising children who are deaf or hard of hearing.

Beginnings—For Parents of Children who Are Deaf or Hard-of-Hearing
800-541-4327
www.beginningssvcs.com
Provides emotional support and access to information for families with deaf or hard-of-hearing children, aged birth through 21.

Hearing Exchange
www.hearingexchange.com
An online community for the exchange of ideas and information on hearing loss. Articles, news, chat rooms, message boards, and parent resources provide interesting and supportive information.

Dogs for the Deaf
541-826-9220
http://www.dogsforthedeaf.org/
Rescues and professionally trains Hearing Dogs to assist deaf people and enhance their lives. The dogs are chosen from adoption shelters, where they might otherwise be euthanized if no homes were found for them.

BOOKS
The Consumer Handbook on Hearing Loss and Hearing Aids: A Bridge to Healing (Second Edition), Richard Carmen, Auricle Ink Publishers, 2004

Luke and His Hearing-Ear Dog, Herald, Andrea Zoll and Arlene J. Garcia, Trafford Publishing, 2004

The Young Deaf or Hard of Hearing Child, Barbara Bodner-Johnson and Marilyn Sass-Lehrer, editors, Paul H. Brookes Publishing Company, 2003

Listen with the Heart: Relationships and Hearing Loss, Michael Harvey, Dawn Sign Press, 2003